Overcoming Abuse:
MY BODY Belongs
to GOD and Me

A Child's Body Safety Guide

Reina Davison

Illustrated by Victoria Aleice

WestBow Press books may be ordered through booksellers or by contacting:

WestBow Press
A Division of Thomas Nelson & Zondervan
1663 Liberty Drive
Bloomington, IN 47403
www.westbowpress.com
1 (866) 928-1240

Interior Image Credit: Victoria Aleice

Scripture taken from the New King James Version®. Copyright © 1982 by Thomas Nelson. Used by permission. All rights reserved.

ISBN: 978-1-9736-7496-2 (sc)
ISBN: 978-1-9736-7497-9 (e)

Library of Congress Control Number: 2019914474

Print information available on the last page.

WestBow Press rev. date: 12/20/2019

WESTBOW
PRESS®
A DIVISION OF THOMAS NELSON
& ZONDERVAN

RELEASE OF LIABILITY

This book has been written with the intent of providing a parent/caregiver a tool to be used as an intervention in helping a child understand the subject of good touch and bad touch (no touch!). If, as a reader, you find this work on teaching children body safety offensive, it may be that you are not the intended audience. This book was not written to be used as a diagnostic tool or to treat body safety problems; consult a mental health or medical provider for diagnostic treatment. The author and publisher are not liable in responsibility for any mental, medical, or economic needs that require professional supervision, and they are not liable for any negative consequences or damages from any exercises, or theological suggestions, to any person reading, listening to, or following the information provided in this book. Resources and references are provided for useful purposes and are information that may change with time and do not constitute endorsement of any organization, website, or other sources.

The content of this book is not to be held as the author's or publisher's endorsement. This work is not a warranty or guarantee or implied belief of the publisher's choice to allow any of the contents in this book. The readers certify and agree that if any difficulty is experienced by portions of this book whereby past trauma is triggered that they will seek support while reading or listening to this book. The reader is responsible for his/her own free-will choice to read the book contents and for any actions as a result of reading this book. Neither the author nor the publisher shall be liable for any personal or otherwise social media comments/reviews, loss, or, injury, or, special, incidental, or consequential damages resulting from a person's choice to read or listen to this book.

The work in this book has been presented solely as an informational and educational source. The author and publisher are not offering a cure-all method for child body safety. Neither the author nor the publisher shall be held liable to any person or entity with respect to alleged libel or alleged invasion of privacy to have been caused indirectly or directly by the information contained in this book.

Any definitions of body abuse or scenarios cited which constitute immoral acts are solely written about for the purpose of information and education. Child body abuse is ungodly. Body abuse in modern society is no different than what is cited in the Bible as the immorality of Sodom, Gomorrah, and Babylon, and that which is spoken of in Judges 19:25, Leviticus 18:6, Deuteronomy 22:25-26, 2 Samuel 13:5-17, and Mark 7:21-22.

There are realities and truths that are the foundation of body abuse and that are against God's moral principles. The author, assistants in publishing, and the publisher do not endorse explicit immoral acts outside of the biblical principles which are consistent with Christian morality. Any discussions of godless behaviors are presented not to have blunt discussions on amoral acts, but to present the truth about body abuse and to offer prevention, possible solutions, God's moral principles, as well as a relationship with Him. The author, those involved in the preparation or publishing of this book, and its publisher assume no responsibility for any reader or listener who chooses to label the contents as impure, obscene, or unholy material. God's Word teaches His people to use wisdom and to teach that wisdom to their children. To deny children wisdom about body safety and not allow them to speak openly when they feel unsafe or to remove the truth about body abuse in children's literature is to invite satan and the abuser to maintain the problem (sin) of unsafe touch in our society.

The author has researched data and sources which are believed to be reliable information that is in accordance with the professional code of ethics and current standards of practice at the time of publication. In the event of the possibility of human error or changes in the medical and mental health sciences, neither the author nor the editor and publisher, or any other parties who were involved in the process or publication of this book guarantees that the information contained in this work is complete and flawless in respect to accuracy and they are not responsible for accidental omissions, errors, or any outcomes which result from the use of the information in this book. Readers are encouraged to consult with Scripture, continue the research contained in this book, and to confirm with additional sources.

To My grandchildren

in this Generation and in the Future Generations

FOREWORD

Marriage and Family therapist, Reina Davison, has written a book that every parent needs in order to prepare their child for life in a world where child sexual abuse is prevalent. It is designed to teach a preschool or elementary-age child that their body is a gift that belongs to only "God and me"!

The author has written this book through the lens of a merciful God who loves children. Parents are given the responsibility to raise their children so they will be prepared to know how to appropriately respond when encountering the advances of a sexual predator.

Parents would rather not have this conversation with their child. Most do not know what they should say, so they often leave this up to school teachers who also may not be prepared to deal with this complex issue.

Overcoming Abuse: My Body Belongs to God and Me is a perfect answer for parents who want to prepare their children who may well face sexual abuse. The book can be read with children and it is written to the child. The first sentence says, "Hello, overcomer child!" You may ask, "Why should my child be called to be an overcomer?"

The term overcomer may sound too strong for a child, but the author goes on to say every child must be an overcomer because there are people who are no touch people! And, there are people who are good touch people! Every child needs to know how to make this distinction for their own safety.

This is especially true because parents cannot always be with their children. When a child is alone, he or she needs to know how to respond to no touch people! That is what this book does. It is a Child's Body Safety Guide. It is a gift to parents and a gift to their children.

I strongly urge every parent to read this book with their children. Every sentence provides parents with an opportunity for meaningful conversation with their children concerning human sexuality. In the process, your child will be taught how to respond to no touch people, something few parents are prepared to teach on their own.

Read this book with your children and you will be raising them up in the way they should go. Nothing could be more important for a parent in today's world.

John K. Graham, M.D., D.Min., MSc., President and CEO
Institute for Spirituality and Health at the Texas Medical Center, Houston, Texas

THANK YOU TO ALL THE PEOPLE
WHO CONTRIBUTED TO THIS BOOK

First off—praise and honor and glory go to my Lord and Savior—Savior of all! It is His Holy Spirit that penned this book and its ministry. Gratitude beyond measure goes to all of the people who conversed with me about the development of this book and those who prayed for its publication. Thank you for your support, insights, and encouragement throughout the publishing process and for joining me on this mission to protect children.

Victoria Aleice, I am certain that you have earned treasures in heaven for applying all of the gifts of art which you have been given...to the illustrations of this book. Thank you for serving Him from the beginning sketches of this project, through those long painting and coloring days and nights, to the very end as you obeyed His calling for the artwork of this book ministry. Victoria Aleice, a personal thank you for joining me as a comrade for the vision and purpose of the book.

Mary Ellis Rice, you were and always will be the first proofreader and editor to each of my books in the Overcoming Abuse book series. From the very beginning when I handed you my manuscripts I knew that they would be treated with respect and that they were in the hands of someone who not only had the skills as a professor of writing but who genuinely cared about the ministry of abuse. Thank you is insufficient; so I will allow the good Lord to bless you in return.

Amy Mize, you too have been a godsend! Words cannot express a thank you for your selfless giving spirit when asked with short notice for your assistance with photography. In spite of your overwhelming life schedule; day or night, you are always ready to supportively assist.

Gabrielle Elizabeth your willingness to sacrifice rest and your personal agenda as a digital media editor was evidenced in the work you were willing to do. Thank you for coming in with your digital heroine cape to follow the Master's calling in the completion of a design team's work!

To all who have labored in the preparation and completion of this book at WestBow Press especially Bob DeGroff. Bob, thank you for your genuine author caring and for your exemplary work ethic, you are an asset to WestBow Press.

Many heartfelt thanks to each of you who invested time reading the manuscripts right before publication and gladly provided your qualitative and quantitative feedback for reviews.

Dr. Graham you have earned a place alongside my family of God circle. In spite of your time demands you willingly accepted the laborious undertaking of reading two manuscripts and caringly wrote a Foreword for each book. Thank you for serving Him through these book projects.

I am grateful for the blessing of my family of origin and my immediate family who has prayed for my books to develop; and for the books to serve God's people. Thank you for patiently standing back and trusting for His work to come to be!

Dear Parent, Grandparent, Caregiver, or Helper,

All children require unlimited nurturing to develop into healthy individuals. Part of nurturing includes being generous with affection. However, smothering children with improper physical affection can become a problem because children have comfort zones just like adults. Your child has a right to decline any physical affection that he's uncomfortable with. This book provides examples of proper and improper affection—good touch and no touch! Your child will learn how to identify no touch people.

When your child is taught that he can *overcome* any troubles, that his body was created by God *and* that it is a special gift from Him, he allows God and himself total ownership of his body. This ownership empowers your child to say "NO!" when a person approaches him with improper affection; it frees him to tell a trusted adult. Validating your child's discomfort with a no touch person also encourages your child to have ongoing trust in you to protect him. This book will help your child to use his/her mind in choosing body safety—so that he/she can live as God intended-*loved-protected—and safe.*

If you have more than one child, read this book individually to each child; this allows you the flexibility to skim read and adjust for reading level and age-appropriateness. Having individual reading sessions provides an opportunity for each child to share openly without concern for the presence of siblings. Some children will require more time to ask questions. Younger children, will need this book to be read in more than one sitting, so that their shorter attention spans can internalize the concepts as a process. As children grow, it is helpful for the book to be re-read periodically until they mature into a full comprehension of God's role, a healthy adult's role, and their own self-protection plan to overcome CSA.

The objective is to have a positive growing experience learning about body safety and to apply the skills learned *if ever* confronted with unwanted body touch. By reading this book with your child and having a discussion based on its contents, you will be able to teach your child prevention and protection from unsafe body touch.

Prepare your reading environment by making it pleasant and distraction-free; this topic is too important to have something or someone interrupt your child's teaching moment. Bring your favorite refreshments to enjoy with your child as you read and begin your journey into preventing and protecting him/her from unsolicited body contact—for a lifetime!

God bless you and your family as you *overcome* and stay safe,

Reina Davison

Hello, Overcomer child!

You're probably wondering why I just called you an Overcomer child. It's because God created you to be an Overcomer! What does it mean to be an Overcomer? The word Overcomer comes from the word "overcome." To overcome means to defeat (stop) the enemy and win; an Overcomer is a winner! Jesus was the first Overcomer on earth. Do you know Who Jesus is? Jesus is God's son. He's the One Who was bullied and beaten here on earth and hung on a cross to die. But Jesus was the winner because He overcame (defeated) the enemy who hung Him on that cross. He *overcame* all His troubles by rising from His death!

In the Bible, Jesus says that even though we may have problems here on earth, we are *not* to have fear; instead, we should live in *peace* because Jesus can *overcome* all the troubles in the world! This is what Jesus says: "These things I have spoken to you, that in Me you may have peace. In the world you will have tribulation; but be of good cheer, I have overcome the world" (John 16:33). Tribulation means the same as *troubles* or *problems.*

It is important to remember what Jesus said because not only did He say to be happy (be of good cheer) that He can overcome *any troubles* in our world, but in the Bible, it also says that God created us in His own Image (Genesis 1:27). That means He made us like a copy of Himself. This also means that all humans were created to be just like Him—Overcomers! Clap your hands right now, or do

a little praise dance, and shout out loud, "YAY! I am a winner—an Overcomer!" Now do you understand why I called you an Overcomer child?

This book is about a problem that the world has. The problem in this world is that there are people who are no touch people. Who are no touch people? I will explain no touch people later. But first, I want to tell you that it is not your fault that the world has this kind of trouble—or these types of no touch people.

Let's begin by talking about the great *fun* God had when He created the world and the first people on earth! God sees *everything* He creates as special. Do you know what He said after He created everything? He was so happy and excited; He said it was "very good!" (Genesis 1:31) God has a plan for His people on earth. It is the same plan He had when He made the first people. He created them to take care of His awesome world (Genesis 1:28), *and* He told the people to treat each other with love (John 13:34). You are one of the special people God has created. The Bible says that

He made each one of us inside our mother's body (Psalm 139:13). Do you know what God said when you were born? He said you were, and still says you are "very good!"

When God created you, He gave you a body with many wonderful parts. Some parts are *inside* your body, and others are *outside* your body. One of those amazing *inside* parts is your *mind.* Your mind is

inside your brain. It is the part of the body that thinks, feels, and makes decisions or choices. Your mind tells you and others what you are thinking and feeling. All people have minds.

Inside our minds is a gift that God gave all humans; it is called *free will*. Free will gives us the right to make our own choices! Can you think of how you have used your *mind* for thinking and feeling today? Can you think about how you have used your free will in making decisions and choices today?

For example, I had a peanut butter and honey sandwich on whole grain bread today. That was my own free will choice. My grandson had a peanut butter sandwich on whole grain bread with *no* honey and *no* crust. My granddaughter had a sun butter sandwich on whole grain bread with *no* honey, and my other grandson did not want a peanut butter or sun butter sandwich. We each used our mind and free will to choose our sandwiches. Isn't it exciting that God gave each one of us the gift of a *mind* and *free will?*

When God gave us the gift of our minds and free will, it was because He loves us. His love is also a gift to us. God would never take back His gift of our minds and free will even if we decide to make bad choices. He would be sad and disappointed if we choose to *sin, but* He would not take His gift of love away from us. What is sin? Sin is when we break God's rules—His commandments. God has rules for our behavior, just like your parent or caregiver has. If you want to know about God's rules, you can read them or someone can read them to you in the Bible in Exodus 20:1–7.

God still loves us even when we choose to sin. He continues to pray that we will someday return to making good choices—because making good choices means being obedient to God's safety rules for us. Why does God wait for us to choose to make good choices? Because God never forces us to do things against our will, even if they are good things that He wants us to do!

Now let's talk about some of the *outside* body parts that God gave you. Most outside body parts can be seen all the time, like your head, face, and hands. The outside body parts, like your knees, legs, and feet, are sometimes covered up by your clothes and shoes. Some body parts are *always* covered by our clothes, like your genitals. What are genitals? The outside boys' and girls' body parts that are between the legs are called *genitals.*

Genitals are also called *private parts* or the *privates.* Dictionary.com says that the word *private* means "belonging to some particular person," and it gives an example, such as *private property.* Private property means something that a person owns. Your genitals are private property because they belong to God, Who made you, and they are a gift to you.

When God created people, He created males (boys) and females (girls). A boy or man (male) has a penis and scrotum for his genitals (his privates). A girl or woman (female) has labia and a vagina for her genitals (her privates). Are you a boy or a girl? Whichever one you are, God said, "*Very good!*" when He made you!

4

Besides giving us minds with free will to make choices and beautiful outside and inside bodies, God also gave us our five senses. Do you know what our five senses are? Can you name each sense that God gave you? Let's point to them as we name them out loud. Ready? *Seeing, hearing, smelling, tasting,* and *touching!*

I am sure you have learned a lot in school about your five senses that you use every day. God is delighted when you can *see* to learn and when you can *see* the fun things you like to watch. God loves it when you can *hear* people talk and when you can *hear* the sounds of your favorite music, games, or movies! He knows the *smells* you don't like and wants you to rejoice in the *smells* that you do like. Sometimes, when we smell something that we like, it makes us smile, like flowers, treats, or food. We usually want to bring that nice smell closer to our noses. If it's our *favorite* food that we smell—yummy!—we want to *taste* it!

We also have the sense of *touch.* We can touch something to know if it is hot or cold; we can touch our toys, books, games, and *everything.* Can people *really* touch everything? No!

Remember: at the beginning of this book, I told you I would tell you later about no touch people. First, let's talk about the two kinds of touch that all people have to choose from. There is good touch, which is the same as God touch. The Bible talks about Jesus touching the little children who came to see Him. "Then they brought little children to Him, that He might touch them ... And He took them up in His arms, laid His hands on them, and blessed them" (Mark 10: 13a, 16).

The other kind of touch is no touch! There are people in this world who do not choose good touch. They do not choose the kind of touch that God wants them to choose. These are the no touch people who bring trouble into the world. What is no touch? No touch is when you say, "No!" to *anybody* who wants to touch you in ways that make you feel scared. Anyone who tries to touch your body when you don't want them to touch you becomes a no touch person in your life.

No touch people want to touch the outer parts of your body (your privates), or they will ask you to touch their outer parts (their privates). No touch is a wrong choice, and it is always the fault and sin of the no touch person. You are never to blame when a no touch person tries to touch you. God has given us His gift of good touch by giving us family, friends, teachers, coaches, caregivers, and many people who can touch us with God touch. It is not part of God's plan for us to feel unhappy when we are touched. God wants us to feel loved when we are touched. God wants you to use your *mind* to choose God touch because it will bring you joy!

Turn to your parent or caregiver right now and share when you have enjoyed good touch. Did you say that you feel good when you are hugged? Maybe you said that you like to snuggle up to read a book or watch a movie with someone. Or perhaps you said that you like to hold hands with your parent or caregiver when you go on walks. How about swinging around the room and holding on to your parents' hands or getting a piggyback ride to bed? I'm sure you have many more ideas for times when you have enjoyed a loving, *good touch!* Loving, *good touch* is part of God's plan for our lives.

The devil wants people to choose no touch! Who is the devil? The Bible says that the devil was the highest of all angels, but because he chose to turn against God, God cast him out of heaven. The devil is an evil angel who now walks around the earth, searching for people whom he can get to disobey God.

The devil disguises himself as a good person so humans can't tell that it's really him—the evil one—trying to get them to sin. If you want to learn more about how the devil tried to trick Jesus into sin and how he wants to do the same to all humans, ask your parent or caregiver to read the Bible to you so you can learn more (Isaiah 14:12–15, Matthew 4:3–10, Job 1:7, 1 Peter 5:8, Revelation 12:7–12).

Today, I want to talk to you about how the devil wants to trick *you* into saying *yes* to a no touch person. No touch is a sin. A no touch person is just like the devil, who wants you to break your safety rules. What are rules? Rules are the guides that children and adults use to choose right from wrong. A guide gives us information and instruction on the *yes* choices and the *no* choices. There are rules (guides) everywhere in our world. This book talks about the most important guide to use in order to choose right from wrong—the Bible.

The Bible has rules on good choices and bad choices. Bad choices are the no-nos. No touch is a no-no. God loves us very much, and because He loves us more than anything else on this earth, He wants us to make good choices—God choices! Good choices keep us safe, healthy, and happy. God is our friend. The devil is our enemy. The devil wants us to make bad choices. The good news is that God is more powerful than the devil, and the Bible says that God has already won the battle with the devil. God is the winner, just like you are!

How can you be ready in case you meet a no touch person? Sometimes, you already know the no touch person. There is no way to *guess* who the no touch people are. There's no way to tell ahead of time who is a no touch person by

the way he or she looks. No touch people can be any age; they can be children, teenagers, young adults, or old adults. No touch people can be boys or girls, men or women.

No touch people can look and act nice, but they have the devil's *way of thinking* and a sin problem. You can't change their sin problem; it's their sin problem, not yours. It is their responsibility to take care of their sin problem. Your only responsibility is to *tell* on no touch people so they won't hurt you or others. The *best* way to take care of the problem of no touch people is to have *no contact* with them. No contact means stay away from them!

It does not matter who the no touch person is; it could be a stranger or someone you know. You can be ready to say, "No!" every day to *any* no touch person by using your mind! When you say, "No!" to no touch, it is the same as using your mind to choose *God touch*.

You have to use your mind to think about whether someone is a good touch or a no touch person. How can you tell if someone is a no touch person? You can tell that *someone is* a no touch person by the way he or she tries to *force* you or trick your mind to get you to let him or her touch your or his or her body parts or privates. God does not want you to *ever* feel bad, confused, hurt, or scared after someone has touched you. If you feel afraid, mixed up, ashamed, or sad after someone has touched you, then it is no touch!

No person has the right—not even family, friends, or caregivers— to scare or hurt you with no touch! What should you do if a no

touch person tries to touch your body? What can you do if a stranger tries to talk to you when you are alone at an activity, or playing outdoors, or walking home from school? Do not answer the person when he or she talks to you. Do not tell the person your name or where you live. If you are in your yard, *run* back into your house, and tell your parent or caregiver. If your parent or caregiver is not inside your home, run to a nearby house (where you can tell that someone is home), and ask for help. Tell your parent or caregiver about the person who tried to talk to you or touch you just as soon as you can!

What if you are home alone, and someone comes to your house and asks you to let him come in for any reason? Say, "No!" because he might be a no touch person. Do not open the door, no matter how kind he sounds. Even if he says he needs help with something, do not let him in. You are a child. Adults can take care of themselves or go get help at another house from another adult. It is not unkind if you do not open the door when you are home alone. It is a smart and safe choice for you. Call and tell your parent or caregiver about that person while he's at the door! If it sounds like he's breaking down the door, call 9-1-1 and talk to the adult. Tell the adult what is happening.

What if a person tries to get you to come into his or her car? Maybe he offers you candy, ice cream, a toy, a puppy, or a nice gift or tries to take you away with him. That is a no touch person. You have to *run* in the opposite direction. You have to find an adult right away! As soon as you see your parent or caregiver, tell him or her quickly what that person said and wanted you to do.

What if a person asks you to sneak out alone with him or her to

9

another room in the house or outdoors somewhere behind the house? That is a no touch person. Run away, and tell your parent or caregiver at once! Tell a trusted adult what he or she wanted you to do. This is important enough for you to interrupt your parent or caregiver to say what happened to you.

What if a person says he wants to show you something in his phone, tablet, computer, magazine, or book, but you will have to keep it a secret? *What if* a person wants to take a picture of you without your clothes on or asks you to take pictures of yourself with no clothes on? Say, "No!" That is a no touch person who uses *bad images* (photos, videos, pictures, or drawings) of children or adults to trick your mind into thinking that he will show you good images—but instead, he shows you bad images. Bad images show the privates. In our world, there's a huge word for bad images: it is *pornography*. People shorten that word and use the word *porn,* which means the same thing—bad images!

Sometimes, children and adults see bad images by accident because the no touch people put them there. You are not bad if you accidently saw a bad image. If you ever accidently see a bad image, there are three things you must do right away! Number one, turn your face away from the bad image. Number two, do an *about-face.* What's an about-face? It's when you turn your body in the opposite direction from where you were facing. Practice that right now with your parent or caregiver. It's like doing a U-turn. Number three, go *quickly* to tell a trusted adult what you saw!

Even though there are bad images, our world is mostly full of *good images* that bring us joy and fun!

There are *super* good images to see everywhere. I *love* to see nature, to look at family photos, and to watch a good movie! What are your favorite good images to see?

I want you to look at the good images of the children in this book, and each time you see a child who's alone, I want you to think about the truth. The truth is that *no one* is *ever* alone. God is everywhere. The Bible says that God watches over us, keeping an eye on the evil and the good (whether we are alone or with our parent or caregiver) (Proverbs 15:3). There are bunches of happy things that we can do when we are with lots of people. But we can also do *many fun things* when we are alone!

Always remember that when you are alone, Jesus is there to talk to (to pray to), and He is there to keep you company. All you have to do is call out His name. You can say, "God" or "Jesus" and then tell Him what's on your mind. God knows all about owies, boo-boos, ouchies, and hurties. Whether you're hurting on your body or in your mind, He wants you to turn to Him for help. His Word (the Bible) encourages you not to be afraid, and it promises you that God will go with you wherever you go and that He will never leave you or forsake you (Deuteronomy 31:6)! The word "forsake" means to abandon. To abandon means to leave completely. God promises *never* to leave you completely alone!

In fact, guess what? Did you know that *you* have your very own personal bodyguard? *God is your personal Bodyguard!* The Bible says, "But the Lord is faithful, who will establish you and guard *you* from the evil one" (2 Thessalonians 3:3). You might think that only a *celebrity* (an important, famous person like the

president, a king, or a queen) has a personal bodyguard. But since *you* are the son or daughter of the King of all kings (Jesus Christ), you are a royal celebrity, a precious prince or princess whom He wants to protect. Pray to God, and ask Him to keep no touch people away from you!

Remember that you can say, "No!" because you have a royal superpower as an Overcomer child of God. If a no touch person tries to touch any part of your body, you can say, "Don't touch me!" or "No! I don't want you to touch me like that!" You can *overcome* no touch! Your mind knows that God did not make people to hurt people. You know that God made people because He loved them. He wants them to love one another and to obey Him. So if a no touch person tries to hurt you with no touch, get away from that person, and go tell your parent or caregiver right away! No touch people hurt God when they try to hurt His people by using the good body parts He created in a bad way. No touch people choose to use God's good gift of touch to frighten and hurt people.

What if you're confused and you don't know if something is *good touch* or *no touch*? It is always no touch if it is *scary* and *hurtful* touch. It is no touch if it *does not* feel good. If it feels *bad,* it is no touch! When you don't like the way someone has touched you, that is a no touch person, and that person is wrong for trying to touch you. It is not your fault that he or she tried to touch you. Anytime that anyone, even family, forces you to do things that you do not understand or touches you and tells you to keep it a secret, it is no touch! Never keep no

touch a secret. Always tell someone you trust, like your parent, teacher, adult friend, or a policeman if someone touches you in a confusing way. If it's a parent or caregiver who touches you with no touch, you *must* tell a trusted adult.

We have talked a lot about *what ifs.* The best way to use our minds to think about what we should do *if* we are around a no touch person *or* when we don't feel safe is to have a safety plan. At the end of this book, I have written out an example of a no touch safety plan. Every family is different, but the plan is usually about the same for all families. You and your family can create your own no touch safety plan according to the ages and special needs of your family. Most important is that your family creates the safety plan so that everyone can be safe from the danger of no touch people and to put a stop to no touch!

Remember: you are an Overcomer, and Overcomers always say, "No!" to no touch people, no matter *who* the no touch people are. Overcomers *know* that they not only have an earthly parent or caregiver to *run* to when they are afraid, but they also have God, Who is always available every moment of the day and night! You know that God is your heavenly Father. He is your parent Who treasures you and watches over you every day. When your earthly parent cannot be with you and you are afraid, the Bible says it's okay to pray to God about *everything.*

Talking to God about your troubles and asking for His help is the same as praying. God is always with you, and when you turn to God for help by praying, He will help you to overcome your fears and heal your hurts.

Say this to yourself: "If it feels bad, then it is no touch! God created my body and gave me the gift of my body for good touch—God touch!" Don't *ever* forget that God *loves you,* and that is *why* He made you and gave you the gift of your body. Your body does not belong to a no touch person. It belongs to God and you! Always remember what the Bible says: "Therefore glorify God in your body and in your spirit, which are God's" (1 Corinthians 6:20b). This means that we are to glorify God with what we choose to do with our bodies. The word *glorify* means to honor. The word honor means to respect. We are to respect God by taking good care of our bodies because our bodies belong to Him. Say this out loud: "My body belongs to *God* and *me,* and no touch *is not* in God's plan for my mind and body!"

You have been using the great gift of your mind to think a lot about the difference between no touch *and* good touch (God touch). You have learned to be wise about no touch! Now, let's focus on the best news. The best news about *touch* is that you can rejoice and feel joyful to learn that almost all touches are good touches—God touches! *YAY!*

The people God created on earth, including your parents, are all His people. God shows His love to us and touches us through His people. He expects the same from us. Because He created our bodies and made us in His Image, He feels that whatever we are doing to our own bodies, we are doing the same to Him and the people He created. Now you can stop reading this book for a moment to praise and thank Him for how much He loves you and for your parents, grandparents, and caregivers who love you so very much that they would tell you about no touch and good touch—God's touch!

Let's end this book by saying a thank-you prayer to God for giving you your mind, your body, and His good touch!

"God, thank You for creating me to be an Overcomer. I feel special because You love me so much that You have given me a superpower to overcome any trouble that I may have! Thank You for my mind and my body and the gift of good touch. I have learned what Your plan is for me and Your people. I now know how You want me to use my mind, body, and sense of touch. I ask You to continue to guide me so that I can make good choices. In Jesus's name, amen."

Goodbye, Overcomer child.

God bless you!

Your friend in Christ,

Reina

Overcomer **Child** No Touch **Safety Plan**

✠ The adults will teach every family member and caregiver about good touch and no touch! Every family member will know what a no touch person is.

✠ Every adult will protect the child by only allowing trusted, screened adults to be the caregivers.

✠ The child will not be left alone at places where there will be an opportunity for a no touch person to abuse the child.

✠ All family members will be allowed to speak up and will be encouraged to tell *right away* when a no touch person has approached them.

✠ A trusted adult will always accompany a child to a *public* restroom or spaces where a no touch person may be present.

✠ Adult family members will model to the child respect for their own bodies.

✠ All family members will be taught to respect each other's body privacy boundaries.

✠ Every family member will knock on a closed door and respect privacy before entering the room. All room doors have to remain open whenever family or friends are visiting.

✠ A child's request not to be touched will always be honored. If a child does not want to be hugged or kissed when greeted or sit on a friend's or family member's lap, the child can say, "No, thank you."

✠ The child will tell the parent or caregiver if there's a person whom they are not comfortable being around. The child will tell the person that they feel uncomfortable; the adult will also let that person know this.

✠ The family will make a list of *trusted* friends whom the child can call if the child has a no touch concern and the parent or caregiver is not available.

✠ The family will create a list of resources that the child can call in the event of a no touch emergency.

RESOURCES

Childhelp USA
National Child Abuse Hotline: **1.800.4.A.CHILD (1.800.422.4453)**
www.childhelpusa.org

Darkness to Light End Child Sexual Abuse
Call **866.FOR.LIGHT** or **text LIGHT to 741741**
https://www.d2l.org/get-help/national-resources/

Stop It Now!®
Office: **413.587.3500**
Helpline: **1.888.PREVENT (1.888.773.8368)**
Email: **helpline@stopitnow.org**
Website: www.stopitnow.org

Protect Young Eyes: Defending Kids from Online Danger
How to Block Porn on Any Device for Free, by Chris McKenna
https://www.protectyoungeyes.com

Stewards of Children® Prevention Toolkit
The *Stewards of Children®* Prevention Toolkit Mobile App can be downloaded for parents and caregivers to learn how to protect their children from sexual abuse.

World Childhood Foundation Inc.
900 3rd Ave. 29th Floor
New York, NY 10022
212-867-6088
info@childhood-USA.org
Mission: To stimulate, promote and enable the development of solutions to prevent and address sexual abuse, exploitation and violence against children.

ANOTHER WESTBOW PRESS BOOK
BY REINA DAVISON

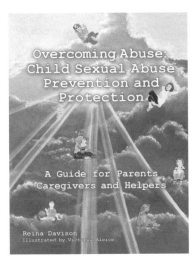

In *Overcoming Abuse: Child Sexual Abuse Prevention and Protection*, author Reina Davison offers an encyclopedic manual for parents, caregivers or helpers to educate their self and train children on body safety. Davison presents a reservoir of information on the dynamics of child sexual abuse, the sex offender profile, and how to protect and prevent a child from being a target of child sexual abuse anywhere, including the internet. It spells out the process of preventing and overcoming child sexual abuse and offers hope and healing. It helps parents, caregivers, and all adults to reassure children that home is where love is, and child sexual abuse is not. To bring the message of *Overcoming Abuse: Child Sexual Abuse Protection A Guide for Parents Caregivers & Helpers* to your organization, church, or event, visit: **www.overcomingabuse.info**

ABOUT THE BOOK

This book provides examples of proper and improper affection and the difference between good touch (God touch) and no touch! The child is taught how to identify a no touch person. Body safety is taught for protection at home, in the community, and on the internet.When your child is taught that he can overcome any troubles, that his body was created by God and that it is an *amazing* gift from Him, he allows God and himself the ownership of his body. This ownership empowers your child to say "NO!" when a person approaches him with improper affection; it liberates him to tell a trusted adult when he feels scared and unsafe. This book will help your child to use his mind in order for him to live as God intended—loved and safe.

Printed in the United States
By Bookmasters